Patty & Rick,

Thank you so very much for all of the help you gave Mom and for being there" for our family. She had a special place in her heart for both of you. This book was written by one of my best friends Mom. He is a pastor in Greensburg. Helen enjoyed this along with her daily prayers. May God's Word bring you PEACE, JOY, BLESSINGS.

Sparkle

Love,

6/18/22

Author, Sheila M. Lauffer

Sheila is a Bible Study Teacher, Sunday School Worker and developer of Church School curricula. Her beloved husband, Clarke H. Lauffer went to be with the Lord in 2011. Their lives, dedicated to The Glory of God and His Word, helped each of the churches they associated with to grow. Sheila is a founding member of Calvary Chapel Westmoreland County, PA, where her son, Clarke, is Pastor. www.calvarychapelonline.com

Mrs. Lauffer loves to teach God's Holy Word, The Bible. Sheila has also shared her ministry at conferences and speaking engagements. During her career as a fashion model she had the blessing of influencing many to seek the Beauty of God in all things. You may contact her through email. lauffercs@aol.com Use, The Sparkle of The Lord, in the subject.

Prologue

That I may publish with the
Voice of thanksgiving
Psalm 26:7

I dedicate this book to my sons, Clarke and Doug, who love and edify me every day.

And, to my sister, Andrina, who has been an inspiration and delight throughout the years!

Introduction

31 Days of Sparkle

This book is for people who like you and me need to keep it together through the **Word of God**.

Sparkle happens when something catches your eye, the flash of a red bird against a blue sky, the sparkle of a diamond on a happy hand, or the excitement on a face when the Holy Spirit reaches a heart. We sparkle when the Lord Jesus Christ shines through us.

"Ye are the light of the world. A city that is set on a hill cannot be hid. Neither do men light a candle, and put it under a bushel, but on a candlestick; and it gives light unto all that are in the house. [16] Let your light so shine before men, that they may see your good works, and glorify your Father who is in heaven."
Matthew 5:14-16

Let's spend some time together.

"The Joy of The Lord is My Strength"
Nehemiah 8:10

What is the joy of the Lord?

"Who for the joy that was set before Him endured the cross."
Hebrews 12:2

His joy was to die for me, for you, on that cross, on that hill known as Calvary. Your strength and my strength, my life and your life began there.

Let's sparkle out our thanksgiving. Let's praise Him every morning and every night for this astonishing love. A love that keeps no record of wrongs. A genuine love that doesn't remember words spoken or words not spoken that should have been, and then, it's too late.

"... love bears all things, believes all things, hopes all things, endures all things..."
1 Corinthians 13:7

We must endeavor to love like our Heavenly Father,

"Who will hurl our iniquities into the depth of the sea."
Micah 7:19

For He calls us His "**Beloved**" and so we are. We read,

"As far as the east is from the west, so far hath he removed our transgressions from us."
Psalm 103:12

He pours the sparkle of love and forgiveness into our lives.

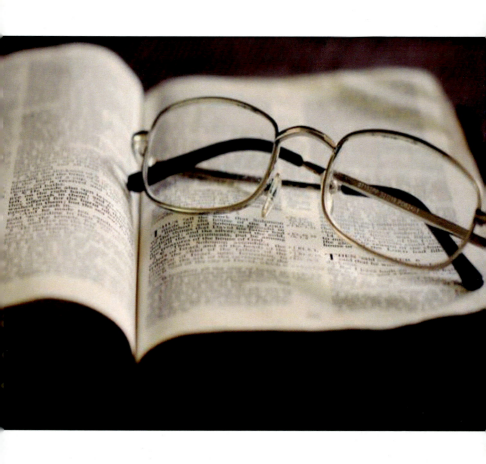

This morning I talked with a friend whose life was coming apart. Some days are like that for all of us, when there doesn't seem to be a sparkle to be found.

But, together we went to the Lord, and He said to us <u>through His Word</u>, "In the world you will have tribulation" (which is sorrow, heartbreak, and "falling apart times"). The second part of this verse says, "But be of good cheer I have overcome the world" (with its sorrow, heartbreak and failing apart times).

The BE OF GOOD CHEER is the sparkle part and we look at **Jesus** and we do. He has filled us once again with His solid words of help and grace to let us know He is with us when we go through the waters. Always He holds our hand, so they don't drown us.

"These things I have spoken unto you, that in me ye might have peace. In the world ye shall have tribulation: but be of good cheer; I have overcome the world."
John 16:33

"When thou passest through the waters, I will be with thee; and through the rivers, they shall not overflow thee…"
Isaiah 43:2

My friend and I received these sparkling words of our Lord and they put us together again!

We have an ever-present God.

"…I am with you always even unto the ends of the earth."
Matthew 28:20

The Lord tells us we are to be content in whatever state we are in; this is easy when we like the state we are in but, the **"whatever state"** may not be to our liking!

"...for I have learned, in <u>whatever</u> state I am, therewith to be content"
Philippians 4:11

Sickness, losing your ability to do what you once did; your strength, "When did that bottle get so hard to open?" You get the picture.

But back in Philippians He said, "all states", that says to me not just the ones we like. I am discontented if I am not content in <u>all</u> states, so therein lies my huge mistake. You know the ones when we murmur and mumble against His ways. I am unhappy with the Lord's will for my life if I struggle where He has put me!

On realizing this mistake, it is time to go to the Lord in prayer, my bad attitude has totally removed my sparkle! Snits always do that.

So I pray. Please Lord help me realize that You put me in <u>all</u> my states; they are a part of Your plan for my life and Your plan is always best for me.

"For I know the plans I have for you, to give you hope and a future."
Jeremiah 27:11

Thank you, Jesus; I feel a very large sparkle coming on.

There was a time in my life when we had clothes for every occasion. Many times, I felt I didn't have the right thing to wear for a special occasion and I would not fit in. Then, I read:

"I will greatly rejoice in the LORD, my soul shall be joyful in my God; for he hath clothed me with the garments of salvation, he hath covered me with the robe of righteousness, as a bridegroom decks himself with ornaments, and as a BRIDE adorns herself with her jewels".
Isaiah 61:10

I realized the Lord has me covered, clothed in the right thing to wear, **"the robe of righteousness"**. His amazing grace covers me, and when I go to be with Him for all eternity I will be sparkling, and I will fit in!

He has seen to every detail. At this special occasion, the Marriage Feast, a banquet like no other, I will be clothed just right, and you will be too.

**And he said unto me, Write, blessed are they which are called unto the marriage supper of the Lamb.
And he said unto me,
these are the true sayings of God.**
Revelation 19:9

We will be sparkling for all eternity.

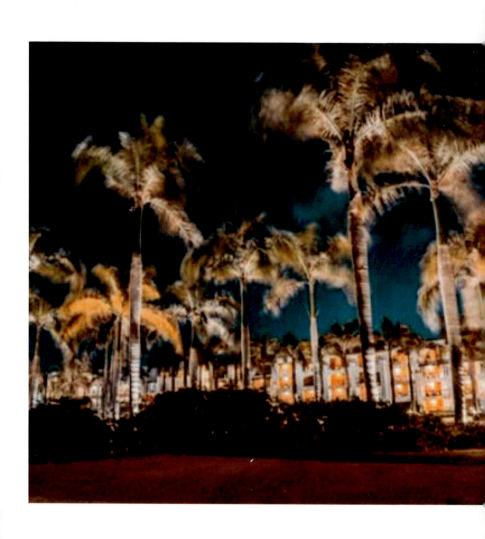

The sparkle in life comes from the joy the Holy Spirit has placed in our spirit, the gift of joy in the midst of great adversity. It bubbles up and keeps us steady, and sparkling, ever-focused on **Jesus**, who gives us strength to endure, to mourn, to recover, when what seems impossible to go through is beating up our hearts. When the loss we are suffering seems unbearable, when we can't face another day and go on with life, then, deep inside comes the voice of our Lord and He says, I will carry you till you can walk again. "Look at Me; I am the Healer of broken hearts, broken dreams, and broken lives. I give hope and the courage to stand up again and go on."

"He heals the broken in heart and binds up their wounds.
Psalm 27:14

**Wait on the LORD: be of good courage, and He shall
strengthen thine heart:
wait, I say, on the LORD."**
Psalm 147:3

Then I know I can sparkle through it all witnessing to His strength and compassion.

We need to remember the Holy Spirit came to live in us. With His gift and His fruit in our lives such as love, peace and patience, these are what make us sparkle.

Jesus enables us to walk in this newness of life and uses these fruits to enable us to live a sparkling life to the praise and the glory of **HIS DIVINE GRACE!**

Today I am feeling insignificant, inadequate and unable to fix myself and certainly I can't fix anyone else! In this place of stifled spirit, it occurs to me that maybe I have assumed the role of the Vine forgetting that I am only a branch! **Jesus is the Vine** and He has said without me you can do nothing.

"I am the vine, ye are the branches: He that abides in me, and I in him, the same brings forth much fruit: for without Me you can do nothing."
John 15:5

I was forgetting this and gradually detaching from the Vine! Busy without His strength or wisdom. He is wisdom.

"For the Lord gives wisdom, out of His mouth comes knowledge and understanding."
Proverbs 2:6

He is sufficient and adequate for anything that should arise. We make the mistake of looking to ourselves. When we seek Him and His strength and His wisdom, we find He pours out His strength and wisdom all over the situation and we begin to sparkle again with His sufficiency. We are now showing that we are a connected branch to the Vine.

"Let the words of my mouth, and the meditation of my heart, be acceptable in thy sight, O LORD, my strength, and my redeemer."
Psalm 19:4

Now, how can we do anything but sparkle?

When someone you consider a friend comes against you and you are reeling from the accusations and crushing words, stumbled by this surprising attack on your integrity, blown away by false reproaches, you find yourself crumbling. You feel so alone, undone and deeply hurt by a friend. With quenched spirit you cry "What to do, what to do?" Then, in a moment of clarity you know that it is the enemy of your soul that has brought this about to come against you as a person, shatter your heart and rob you of the Lord's help.

Then, you know what to do. You must go to your defender, and cry unto the Lord, the Holy One who will keep you once again from sliding farther into the pit of despair.

"Blessed be the LORD, because he hath heard the voice of my supplications."
Psalm 28:6-7

As you cry to Him once again, you find the Lord is your strength and your shield.

"The LORD is my strength and my shield; my heart trusted in him, and I am helped: therefore, my heart greatly rejoices; and with my song will I praise him."
Psalm 28:7

Our spirit lifts, as He sends the sparkle of His words that comfort and heal us. You know there will be a time when you can share them back and they will sparkle into another's life who is going through betrayal.

I have a close friend of many years and through the years I have seen her deep compassion for others as she prays for them and many times, with them.

Her witness as a follower and disciple of Christ, is truly a visible sparkle as she helps and encourages others. Her example shows a strong desire to follow God's Word and she puts her life in His Hands trusting Jesus and His truth. Her faith is constantly developing and is consistent as a source of sharing the love of **Jesus** to the weak and fearful. His grace sparkles out of her.

"By grace you are saved..."
Ephesians 2:8

Sometimes as prayers are made, people are healed. A miracle is witnessed; but always they are comforted. God's love is seen through her caring and tenderness.

She is trusting His Word and learning He is in charge of everything. As she reads His Word her faith and ours will always grow. Her sparkle shows as she shares with others what she is learning from the Lord. She gives to others the fruit of His Spirit.

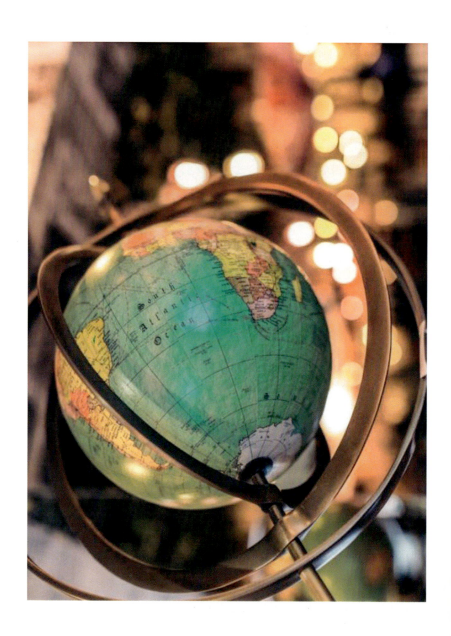

It says in the Word,

"In Him dwells all the fullness of the Godhead bodily, and you are <u>complete</u> in Him"
Colossians 2:9

As I read these words I realized I have been feeling so, so incomplete! Nothing seemed to be going right, at least not my way. Things seemed out of balance. I felt weak and discouraged, no sparkle. You have been here too, I am sure, when our human weakness gets the best of us and the worst can take over. We cry out, "WHERE ARE YOU?"

Finally, I begin to walk through the pages of His Word and I come to:

"The earth is the Lord's and the fullness therein, the world and <u>all</u> that dwell in it."
Psalm 24:1

That is you and me, we are the "all". Then I know in due time HE will fill me up and for right now "I AM COMPLETE IN HIM"!

BINGO, suddenly I come back focused on the LORD and all He is and His completeness! His sparkle is within me and my spirit is revived. The sparkle is back. LET'S sing glory to God as we praise His completeness in you and me!

Today I am faith leaking, sparkle lacking, I have a hole in my cup and the living water is running out, what is the problem?

My faith is fading, what can I do? Then, I remember that

"Faith comes by hearing and hearing by the Word of God."
Romans 10:17

<u>Hearing</u> not just reading, I have forsaken the church and the gathering of His people. There at church is the preaching of <u>His Word</u>.

"Not forsaking the assembling of ourselves together, as the manner of some is…"
Hebrews 10:35

"The church is full of hypocrites" is my excuse. We have all heard this many times as an excuse for not attending church. But, I know they are just people, like me. We are imperfect and seeking a perfect God, and I am brought to my knees. My reason for being in church is to worship the King of Kings, to hear His Word spoken and to embrace people who need His special love as I do!

Here I shall be refreshed by His Word spoken out loud. Then, I can sparkle to others with His love, forgiveness and grace and how He restores us in the midst of such mistaken thinking. We are to know Him in the BEAUTY of His Holiness.

**"Give unto the LORD the glory due unto his name;
worship the LORD in the beauty of holiness."**
Psalm 29:2

**"I was glad when they said unto me, Let us go into the
house of the LORD."**
Psalm 122:1

The sparkle of the Lord is going home with me.

I heard a bird sing today and it brought to my mind, "I sing because I'm happy, I sing because I'm free! His eye is on the sparrow and I know He watches me."

How wonderful that I am being watched by the Creator of the universe and Creator of you and me and that little sparrow. How He tells us in His Wonderful Word that we are infinitely important to Him; **"He counts the hairs on our head"** and **"He sees each sparrow that falls."**

> **"But even the very hairs of your head are all numbered. Fear not therefore: ye are of more value than many sparrows."**
> Luke 12:7 Jesus

He shows me that every detail of His creation is so important, and <u>all is in His care</u>. My finite understanding helps me see the significance of this and makes me realize that I can trust Him for every detail of my life, large or small.

I can sparkle with the assurance of how much He cares for me. Out into the world, my world and your world, I am singing His praises, His eye is on me. I have a glimpse of God's infinite mind and the significance of His sparkling forever promises!

JOHN 3:

be lifted up, [15] that whoever believes in him may have eternal life." [16] For God so loved the world that he gave his only Son, that whoever believes in him should not perish but have eternal life. [17] For God sent the Son into the world, not to condemn the world, but that the world might be saved through him. [18] He who believes in him is not condemned, he who does not believe is condemned already, because he has not believed in the name of the only Son of God. [19] And this is the judgment, that the light has come

I read in Jeremiah today**,**

"I have loved you with **an everlasting love, therefore with loving kindness I have drawn you."**
Jeremiah 31:3

It is the loving kindness of the Lord that will bring people to Him. We must remember this love when we are behaving judgmentally or acting superior or feeling "better than", when we are dealing with someone who needs the love of the **Lord**, just as we did. What we've received from Jesus wasn't because of any special redeeming qualities that we had in us. My sparkle came because he filled me with **His** love <u>freely</u>.

He became my Savior just as I was, a sinner saved by grace. My thanksgiving and His sparkle touch every inch of me. **"My cup runneth over"** for I see this deep and abiding love He has for all of us.

**"For God so loved the world He gave His only Son that whoever believes in Him
will not perish but have everlasting life."**
John 3:16

When we believe this, the Father accepts us where we are <u>**unconditionally**</u>, and we know His Son did it all and we are now one of His precious sparkling sheep.

Today I am in the garden where I talk with You and hear Your wisdom so clearly for my life. You tell me about the soil of the garden and how preparing it properly with the right nutrients makes for a strong garden.

This is like life and sometimes I am not properly prepared. I run ahead unprepared all by myself taking short cuts and making rash decisions. Later I know things would have gone so much better had I waited on You to lead me, I would have been better prepared.

Oh, how foolish we are to think that we can do life without YOU!

When we pray for anything, first we should let You prepare the soil for whatever we are going to do or with whomever we are going to be meeting. We should be well prepared in You so that we can sparkle with Your good preparation for this time and You will be in the midst. Then, You will be seen and perhaps come into an empty heart and parched soul.

Your instructions for preparing us will bring life.

"The preparations of the heart in man, and the answer of the tongue, is from the LORD."
Proverbs 16:1
Oh, how we sparkle when we go into everything with Him.

This morning I watched a robin picking up more grass than he could handle, it took him a while to realize he would have to leave some of it and come back later for some more. And, he did again and again until he had it all. This is so like me to pick up and take on more that I can handle and wonder why I am feeling so stressed and out of sorts!

We could do so much more if we did it in "manageable increments" like the robin who came back several times. But, by the end of the day the nest was built. My job could take longer but in time doing it God's way, I will finish what I need to do.

Thou hast enlarged my steps under me
that my feet did not slip.
Psalm 18:36

I need to learn not to take on what is too much for me. No is a word that I seldom use. Busy people many times are yes people. Don't quench your sparkle; say no sometimes relax and rejoice in a life of more of what the Lord wants us to do. He wants us to know Him better, praise Him more and remember that His burden is light.

"For my yoke is easy, and my burden is light."
Matthew 11:30
Limitations, we must learn; know **His** manageable increments!

Here is something to ponder.

"What is man that You are mindful of him…?"
Psalm 8:4
But You called me beloved.

"The LORD God is my strength You make my feet like deer's feet and "make me to walk upon high places."
Habakkuk 3:19

As I read Your words, Your glory breaks forth and sparkles all around me. You are **mindful of me** and You are touching my life, filling me from all directions. My spirit soars and sparkles; Your presence brings me safety in the midst of what seems impossible or unable to be fixed. He is the God of the impossible!

But Jesus beheld them, and said unto them, with men this is impossible; but with God all things are possible.
Matthew 19:26

When problems and disappointments are all around me, then another important discovery is made. I see my disappointments are "me-made"! They are brought on by anticipating something ahead of time or wanting things to work out according to my way. I forget that my thoughts are not your thoughts and my ways are not your ways.

"For my thoughts are not your thoughts, neither are your ways my ways, says the LORD."
Isaiah 55:8

I have developed in my mind a whole picture of what should be. I must step back and wait on You Lord to solve the problems and change the disappointments. And, as I magnify the Lord and as I listen to <u>Him</u>, He brings the sparkle that cheers and comforts my being; and it spills out again for His glory!

He is the God of the impossible in Him,

"all things are possible!"
Matthew 19:26

When hard lasts and lasts I need to stay in His Word. It doesn't always agree with my thoughts on how I think things should go, but, I know it is the truth.

"Thy word is truth."
John 17:17

His Word is that <u>perfect</u> kind of advice we need, unless we are stubborn or foolish. But, if His advice is taken it keeps us where the Lord wants us to be. When I was going through many years of hard times, it was the Word that sustained me. God's Word showed me my life is not always about me but His purposes.

He showed me I should look out and around me seeing the hurting ones. He showed me that my prayers aren't always answered my way because they may not be according to <u>His will</u>. Sometimes my will sneaks in,

"And this is the confidence that we have in Him, that, if we ask any thing according to <u>His will</u>, He hears us…"
1 John 5:14.

Through it all there was my peace. As hard went on and on I could sparkle because He was holding me up, with His arms and sometimes covering me with His feathers.

"He shall cover you with His feathers and under His wings shall you trust, His truth shall be your shield."
Psalm 91:4

"Even there shall thy hand lead me, and thy right hand shall hold me."
Psalm 139:10

How personal is our Lord Jesus! The steadfast love of the Lord never changes, His mercy never comes to an end and His mercies are new all of the time.

"They are new every morning: great is thy faithfulness."
Lamentations 3:23

This is sparkling news!

"Be ye kind one to another forgiving one another even as God for Christ's sake has forgiven you."
Ephesians 4:32

Every time I read this I bow my head in shame; I know there is

no way I can justify not forgiving anyone for anything.

Unforgiveness can develop a root of bitterness in our spirit.

"Looking diligently lest any man fail of the grace of God; lest any root of bitterness springing up trouble you…"
Hebrews 12:15

This will shut out **"the light of world"**, and our sparkle will

leave us. The Letter of James tells us we cannot be double

minded and be sparkling for the Lord.

"A double minded man is unstable in all his ways."
James 1:8

Because of **Jesus'** sacrifice we have been totally and

completely forgiven for anything and everything. Now, all I

have to do is sacrifice my pride, not my life, when I do this I

release a bad attitude and then, I no longer block the sparkle of

the Lord coming through me.

I cannot call myself a Christian if there is unforgiveness in my heart towards another. Then, I am only "a do as I say, not as I do" hypocritical person.

I will forever remember, You, Lord Jesus, died for my forgiveness!

That was the pouring of Your sparkling right into my heart.

In Luke 5:1 the people pressed in upon Him to hear the Word of God. Further on in Luke 5:18 His fame had spread abroad to the multitudes, and they came together to hear Jesus as He spoke the Word. Jesus was received everywhere by the people as shown by their praises and how they glorified Him. The people said,

"Blessed be the king that comes in the name of the Lord".
Luke 19:38

Next, we see the fickleness of the people in Luke chapter 23 for soon the same people were crying out "CRUCIFY HIM, CRUCIFY HIM!"

So, like us, one minute we love Him and the next minute we hate Him! And most of the time it is because Jesus doesn't give us what we want! We are a people with huge appetites for things that aren't good for us. In our **finite** wisdom we think we should have them. God in His **infinite** wisdom keeps them away from us for they would be wrong for us. Sometimes He doesn't heal someone we love, and they die and we blame God.

I am glad that God is not at my beck and call; I would make a mess of things. He is in charge and what He does is always for His glory and our good.

"And we know that all things work together for good to them that love God, to them who are the called according to His purpose."
Romans 8:28

This is hard to understand; but, to reject Him and His Word is to lose what makes us sparkle.

"I am the way the truth and the life…"
John 14:6

I'm hanging on tightly to the wisdom of God, the all-caring, the all-knowing!

"…for the Lord God omnipotent reigns."
Revelation 19:6

I have heard people referring to a Godsend; "he is a Godsend it was a Godsend." I am pondering what does that mean? I'm thinking it is like a cup of cold water in a time of a thirsty need. Jesus has told us we are lights of the world in Matthew 5:14. We are little ones guided by "The Big One".

I am the light of the world: he that follows me shall not walk in darkness but shall have the light of life.
John 8:12

When we are following Him, He cares for us, encourages us, and gives us hope. He teaches us to be able to do this with others, bringing the living water into a situation. And we sparkle like sun-lit water.

Our sparkle comes from His presence in us. **His** word that encourages us and then is spoken from us will bring His light to others. I know His word encourages my heart and gives a sparkle to my countenance.

"… freely ye have received, freely give."
Matthew 10:8

This is what describes a Godsend to me; something or someone that brings encouragement at the moment we need it. Jesus gives us rivers of sparkling, living water pouring into us like the woman at the well.

"Jesus answered and said unto her, If thou knew the gift of God, and who it is that said to thee, Give me to drink; thou would have asked of him, and he would have given thee living water."
John 4:10

Because to have that living water sparkling in us means we can **"Enter into His gates with thanksgiving and into His courts with praise."**
Psalm 100:4

God has placed us in families for our safety. Sometimes we have a family meeting where we come together to help a member we can see is heading for trouble. We come humbly with love, concern and compassion, like only a family can have toward one another. Where there is wise counsel in the midst, danger can be avoided. Our concern is their vulnerability; they have allowed themselves to be open to the enemy's fiery darts.

"Above all, taking the shield of faith, wherewith ye shall be able to quench all the fiery darts of the wicked."
Ephesians 6:16

As the children of God, we are to be loving, caring and kind but, also, we are to,
"Be wise as serpents and gentle as doves,"
Matthew 10:17.

Jesus said that we are to be discerning of those who may be wolves in sheep's clothing;
"Beware of false prophets, which come to you in sheep's clothing, but inwardly they are ravening wolves."
Matthew 7:15

We must be aware of those that may be trying to stumble us. As we share our concern gently and lovingly, giving warning and advice and if they are received with a humble heart and a thankful and grateful spirit, the Lord's awesome presence falls on us all! There is sparkle all around and our thanksgivings becomes praises and hallelujahs to His glorious name!

"Where no counsel is, the people fall but, in the multitude of counselors there is safety."
Proverbs 11:14

In our family, a member has had a double transplant, a liver and a kidney were received. Keeping this in mind when a tough situation comes up, I say, "Oh well it's NOT a transplant!"

Now the way I see things, has taken on a whole new light. I watched trust, faith and hope at work through many years of waiting for the organs needed for life. I also saw the pain and the sickness, the dramatic breaking down of the body… through it all I have witnessed the WILL TO LIVE. I have seen the struggle to fight for each day of life.

Because of much time with the Lord in His word-when God's word is read over and over His words are really understood, and clearly what they mean. Because again and again they are read and believed with the whole mind and heart. Then, as death comes closer and closer you can stand firm. When negative thinking starts to come into your thoughts, you can remember to let the Lord handle this new assault.

Now when I face a tough situation, I remember this situation is NOT a transplant and the sparkle of Christ's assurance comes back strong and sure!

"Let us draw near with a true heart in full assurance of faith…"
Hebrews 10:22

We sparkle, and The Lord is magnified! [1]

"O Magnify the Lord with me and let us exalt His name together."
Psalm 34:3

---

[1] This transplant surgery was for a liver and a kidney and we are continuing to trust the Lord daily in his recovery.

When something in our life casts a pale shadow over everything and we find ourselves in the dark night of grieving, no one knows broken hearts like Jesus.

Meanwhile we mourn and cry out and won't be comforted. We need help, and no one can help us, can say the right things, or do the right things. Only our Lord has the mercy and comfort we need.

When my spirit fails within me and I am utterly lost I reach out and find You are holding me Lord Jesus! Then, I know You will be with me through this dark time and when I am ready You will begin the healing of my heart. Slowly You will bring me into the light once more restoring my spirit and I know your Spirit within me is everlasting. You are lifting me up flooding me with mercy, comfort and love.

As I come out of the dark night, I know I will sparkle again. Then, Your mind-healing presence in me will sparkle out for others who need to know this truth.

"I sought the LORD, and he heard me, and delivered me from all my fears."
Psalm 34:4

We are not destroyed by the dark night that comes to all of us because this is a part of life, and He is life-giving!

"In Him was life, and the life was the Light of men."
John 1:4

A heart-breaking time has come back into your life. A problem that has circled for years has returned, escalating into such brokenness for everybody. Addiction is an illness that is very hard to treat and it breaks out even when it seems under control. Is it ever truly under control?

Such a damaging sickness that pulls so many into its downward spiral. Wives, mothers, friends, entire families, so many hearts are broken by this terrible trap. Only focusing on the Lord can set us on the rock that keeps the swirling black waters of anxiety, worry, and fear from overwhelming us. This anxiety, worry and fear can't reach us if we are looking to Jesus. We know our only hope lies in His power. As we sparkle out this message it can reach those in addiction and those whose hearts are breaking.

My flesh and my heart fail: but God is the strength of my heart, and my portion forever."
Psalm 73:26

So, we pray they will find comfort, release and deliverance in Jesus' great love, power and steadfastness.

"He that dwells in the secret place of the most High shall abide under the shadow of the Almighty. I will say of the LORD, He is my refuge and my fortress: my God; in him will I trust. Surely he shall deliver thee…"
Psalm 91:1-3

Then the heaviness can lift, and sparkle can return with the knowledge of God's supernatural power!

When I look out at my garden and enjoy the beauty, the many colors, the different shades of green… from a distance it is lovely. Now if I go closer and inspect it, I see weeds beginning to choke things out and the beginning of danger. I see something is eating some of the various plant leaves but, even worse, the emerging buds on another plant won't become flowers unless the source of the danger is found and dealt with…

As the gardener this is my job in my garden. As the Master Gardener my heavenly Father has the same job with me. The weeds of discontent and bad attitudes can be choking out my sparkle. The path I should be walking on may be grown over, choked out and I can't find my way. Unforgiveness may be eating my leaves and flower buds and these dangers are ruining my relationship with Jesus.

It is in His power to fix me if I yield my discontent, bad attitudes, and unforgiveness to Him. This must take humbleness on my part; He loves a humble spirit and contrite heart.

"The sacrifices of God *are* a broken spirit: a broken and a contrite heart…"
Psalm 51:17

His part to fix me and what He gives me to fix me is love, forgiveness and mercy. That brings sparkle to the garden THAT IS ME.

The Lord is our perfect Gardener!

Has anyone mentioned you glow? You should glow because of the living water in you which is like the sparkle on the ocean when the sun hits it. The Son of God has hit you and life has come into you with a new heart;

"A new heart also will I give you, and a new spirit will I put within you…"
Ezekiel 36:26

And, His Holy Spirit now dwells with and in you.

"But ye are not in the flesh, but in the Spirit…"
Romans 8:9

You have become a new creation.

"Therefore, if any man be in Christ, he is a new creature…"
2 Corinthians 5:17

Our way of seeing things now is through the eyes of Jesus. Gentle, loving, merciful… we look beyond the surface of people and we wonder what is happening inside that makes people the way they are? Is it loneliness, heartache, anger, unforgiveness, do they know our Savior? Do they know Jesus Christ and what He said?

"…I am come that they might have life, and that they might have it more abundantly."
John 10:10

Maybe they know the first part, but do they know the second part, to have life and to have it more abundantly?

What is it to have and access <u>the abundance</u>? Abundance comes as we get to know Him more intimately, and when we understand His resources and learn from Him how to use them in this life, our life that He has given us.

"O the depth of the riches both of the wisdom and knowledge of God!"
Romans 11:33

This is a cause for celebration, to be sent out into the world; and we glow, and we have lots of sparkle too!

Are you in a place in your life that you don't like? But, the Lord has put you there. Maybe you have prayed for something and you don't like how He has answered with the gift He has given you! It's not exchangeable and you can't return it. So how can you work through the attitude of discouragement that is a part of not liking what He has given you?

This is going to be a three (3) step program. The first step is realizing this has come from God in answer to your prayer. He has given it to you. So we need to get rid of our bad attitude about this gift.

> **Every good gift and every perfect gift is from above, and cometh down from the Father of lights, with whom is no variableness, neither shadow of turning."**
> James 1:17

The second step then must be changing our attitude to one of acceptance. Then He can change our hearts so that gradually down the road we will like this gift.

The third step will then follow spontaneously, as we accept this gift, we will be thanking Him. We are sending the fragrant sweet-smelling aroma of our love to Him, our offering of thanksgiving.

"For we are unto God a sweet savor of Christ"
2 Corinthians 2:15.

The only sacrifice we can make is to trust Him, accepting what He gives to us as <u>perfect</u>. We understand that He loves us and He is taking care of us.

So then, we sparkle right where He places us.

"And now Lord what wait I for, my hope is in You."
Psalm 39:7

The other day I broke something valuable and needed super glue to put it back together. I arranged the pieces, so they would go together like they were before they broke. With no disrespect, I thought about the Lord and how He is my super glue, He holds me together when I am coming apart. When my day is full of scattered pieces, He will bring to it a sense of order in the midst of the turmoil.

When my heart is torn apart and I am struggling with deep sadness He gathers the pieces together. When my heart within me fails:

"From the end of the earth will I cry unto thee, when my heart is overwhelmed: lead me to the rock that is higher than I."
Psalm 61:2

I know it's to Jesus I need to go because I have learned only He can fix me. There will be a slight scar, but battles will leave scars, we have been there and have come through it alive! How? We find where our help comes from:

"My help cometh from the LORD, who made heaven and earth."
Psalm 121:2

You may be in a battle like I was. So, I tell you this, I am not held together by super glue, it is by the Lord's supernatural love blessing me so that I can share with you how He has once again brought sparkle back into my life!

"That they may see, and know, and consider, and understand together, that the hand of the Lord hath done this, and the Holy One of Israel hath created it."
Isaiah 41:20

Change happens to us all every day. We change, we just don't notice it till one day we do! We perhaps can't walk as far, golf as long, paint a room in one day, run upstairs, or get up and go as quickly. We seem to have less strength to stand for hours at a golf tournament or shop all day. We don't like this and we want things to be like they were. We exercise, we take pills, and we moisturize more trying to get back to what we were. But, our physical bodies are moving on despite all these things we are trying.

We need to accept that we can't change back to the things we once did and once were. Let's be thankful for the things we still can do.

"In everything give thanks: for this is the will of God in Christ Jesus concerning you."
1Thessalonians 5:18

We can't let cravings for the past intrude on our present. The Lord tells us forget what is behind.

"…forgetting those things which are behind, and reaching forth unto those things which are before…"
Philippians 3:13

This includes not just bad or ruined things but many of the good things too. We have spent precious time trying to change the things we can't. Let's look at our walk with the Lord and see that we need some significant changes here, beginning with my attitude toward change that I am not accepting. As I pray for help, You show me, we move on in this life, on Your path.

"You are a lamp unto my feet and a light unto my path."
Psalm 119:105.

Jesus, in You we can be enabled to accept our limitations. You pour over me the sparkle of Your understanding, help and everlasting love. Jesus, make me grateful for what I have. I know Your joy and peace are always with me at all times, even into old age. Amen

"Those that be planted in the house of the LORD shall flourish in the courts of our God. They shall still bring forth fruit in old age; they shall be fat and flourishing;"
Psalm 92:13-14

O, how we can sparkle when we know this truth!

One of the most familiar Psalms in the Bible is Psalm 23. It tells me that the Lord is my shepherd and it goes into detail about how He takes care of me. When He leads me beside the still waters and makes me to lie down in green pastures, He is keeping me safe and giving me rest. When I walk through the valley of the shadow of death, I remember that You are with me. I won't get stuck there, You lead me through or take me up; either is a win-win for I am in the paths of righteousness, saved and forgiven. These promises bring a sparkle to my spirit.

We read "surely goodness and mercy shall follow me <u>all</u> the days of my life". Just see how the good shepherd cares for us! Then, we read we will live in His house forever; that's a promise He is telling me and He keeps His promises!

"For all the promises of God in Him are yes, and in Him Amen, unto the glory of God..."
2 Corinthians 1:20

All that is required of me is to believe and trust in Jesus the Son of God,

"That if thou shalt confess with thy mouth the Lord Jesus, and shalt believe in thine heart that God hath raised him from the dead, thou shalt be saved. For with the heart man believeth unto righteousness; and with the mouth confession is made unto salvation."
Romans 10:9-10

This is a Sparkling promise!

When I read Hebrews chapter 11, the names of the giants of faith, I come to the unnamed ones, "the others". We read about them in verses 36 and 37:

"…being destitute, afflicted, tormented; (Of whom the world was not worthy)"
Hebrew 11:36-37

These people stood up for their faith and were also counted as people of God. They died for the Gospel truth; they spread it and their faith through grace set the world on fire with the good news of Jesus Christ.

This word of God has never been stopped. Because just ordinary people filled with the Spirit of God continue to speak it and the sparkle of their witness is seen all over the world, presenting Jesus through His word.

But then suddenly I feel weak when I read about a famine regarding not hearing the Word of the Lord:

"Behold, the days come, says the Lord GOD, that I will send a famine in the land, not a famine of bread, nor a thirst for water, but of hearing the words of the LORD:"
Amos 8:11

I am afraid for those who haven't met Jesus through His word. Then, I remember that He is not willing that any should perish, and we can trust Him to reach those who will come to Him.

"For God so loved the world He gave His only Son that whoever believes in Him will not perish but have everlasting life."
John 3:16

There will always be people who will keep the fire of His word burning into the hearts of those who will hear.

Oh Lord, I want to be one who will stand up and tell the good news of the gospel, to those who don't know You. You are the God of all hope; You can fill them with all joy and peace when they believe and trust in You.

We can sparkle our witness to the world.

"Now the God of hope fill you with all joy and peace in believing, that you may abound in hope, through the power of the Holy Ghost."
Romans 15:13

The Holy Spirit is teaching me that it's through the power of His word that brings people into the wonder of Him who is called Jesus, the name that sparkles like a laser-beam.

I am having one of those "Lord I believe, help my unbelief"
days. I need you to take me out of this gray place I am in. I
don't know what's wrong, but you do. I don't feel loved. How
foolish this is? I know your love surrounds me!

**"Yea, I have loved thee with an everlasting love: therefore,
with lovingkindness have I drawn thee."**
Jeremiah 31:3

This certainly is sparkle!

This is a start out of the gray place. Then I remember after a
night of darkness, joy comes in the morning and, I read this in
Peter:

**"Whom having not seen, you love; in whom, though now
you see him not, yet believing, you rejoice with joy
unspeakable and full of glory:"**
1 Peter 1:8

Although I don't see You, as I read Your word I am beginning
to "see". You are coming alongside me in this place I am in…
The gray is beginning to lift as I continue to read.

I am encouraged to seek You with my whole heart.

"Sometimes" I lose You, Jesus, and this is what I should do,
seek you! Your word says that I will find You.

"And you shall seek me, and find me, when you shall search for me with <u>all</u> your heart."
Jeremiah 29:13

It is with everything that is in me, I should seek Jesus. And, I will find Him!

Lord, I want You to fill me with what satisfies me. I don't always know what that is. I know You know that it is spending time with You. In all I do and think You are my strength, safety, my security, You have saved me, You are my Savior.

"And my spirit has rejoiced in God my Savior."
Luke 1:47

I have now come out of that gray place I've been in and now I can sparkle in my mind and spirit. I have been filled with You. I've stood on Your words,

"Christ in me the hope of glory"
Colossians 1:27

And, the gates of hell cannot prevail against the truth, Jesus said,

"Thy word is truth."
John 17:17.

"The name of the LORD is a strong tower: the righteous runs into it and is safe."
Proverbs 18:10

Epilogue

Sometimes I forget that my sins are forgiven because sinfulness is still happening in my life. Many times, a day I come to Him and confess my sins of irritation, unthankfulness, meanness and lack of trust / faith. But, I know that He is faithful to forgive me:

"If we confess our sins, He is faithful and just to forgive us…"
1 John 1:9

God can't love me any more than He already does right now! I am covered by the blood of Jesus. **Oh, what a sparkling truth!** This is peace, this is joy and He has given this to you and to me; don't let this assurance be taken away, or it will dry up our sparkle.

Page 102

"The LORD is my shepherd; I shall not want. He makes me to lie down in green pastures: he leads me beside the still waters. He restores my soul: he leads me in the paths of righteousness for his name's sake. Yea, though I walk through the valley of the shadow of death, I will fear no evil: for thou art with me; thy rod and thy staff they comfort me. Thou preparest a table before me in the presence of mine enemies: thou anointest my head with oil; my cup runneth over. Surely goodness and mercy shall follow me all the days of my life: and I will dwell in the house of the LORD forever."

Psalm 23